CHINESE COOKING
FAMILY STYLE

COMPILED BY LILY GER

HEIAN

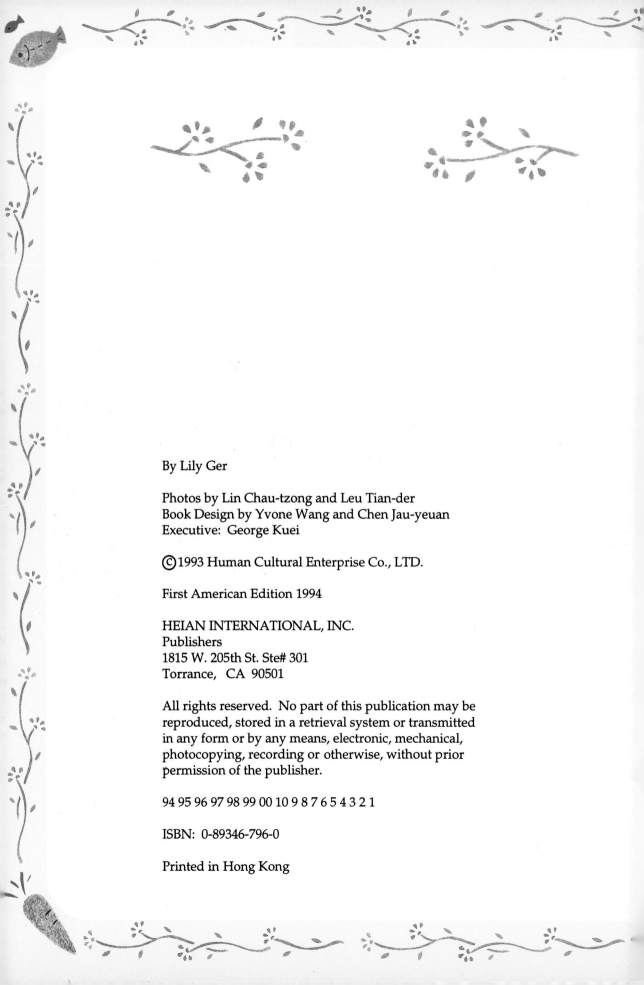

By Lily Ger

Photos by Lin Chau-tzong and Leu Tian-der
Book Design by Yvone Wang and Chen Jau-yeuan
Executive: George Kuei

© 1993 Human Cultural Enterprise Co., LTD.

First American Edition 1994

HEIAN INTERNATIONAL, INC.
Publishers
1815 W. 205th St. Ste# 301
Torrance, CA 90501

94 95 96 97 98 99 00 10 9 8 7 6 5 4 3 2 1

ISBN: 0-89346-796-0

Printed in Hong Kong

CONTENTS

CONTENTS

CONTENTS

Beautifying Your Kitchen

It is common knowledge that one's surroundings can contribute a great deal to one's enjoyment of a meal. That is why people are attracted to pleasantly decorated restaurants. Anyone can strive to create the same atmosphere in their own home.

A tablecloth can help to make an ordinary dining table look elegant and gracious, and it can even whet the appetite. Generally, tablecloths today are either made of plastic or cloth. A plastic tablecloth is easily maintained and kept clean while fabric tablecloths require more frequent washing. However, the latter are usually more conducive to creating a pleasant atmosphere.

Use a tablecloth and potted flowers to create a cozy dining atmosphere.

Plants and Flowers

Flowers and greenery help to make a home stylish. A potted plant or vase of flowers on the dining table provide stimulation for both the eyes and the palate.

Flowers may be fresh, dried, or made of silk. Among such decorative house plants, there are many that are colorful and easy to care for.

Silk flowers are perfect for decoration.

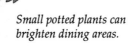

Small potted plants can brighten dining areas.

Planning Your Kitchen

Making full use of available space and arranging utensils according to need will result in a tidy kitchen.

Dishes and Pots

Keep bowls and dishes in cabinets so that they will not collect dust. Seldom-used bowls and dishes may be stored in bags and kept in less accessible cabinet spaces.

Frequently used pots and pans can be hung on the wall while others may be stored in cabinets under the counters. Small cooking utensils can be hung from the kitchen wall where they can be both handy and decorative.

Use the cabinets under the sink efficiently.

Pots may be hung on the wall.

Small utensils on the wall are decorative and useful.

*...our most frequently used ingredi-
...a basket where they are handy.*

...your knives in a knife block on the counter.

Keep cutting boards clean and dry.

*Label your
ingredient
containers to
distinguish them.*

Ingredients

Frequently used ingredients such as salt, soy sauce, flour and cornstarch should be easily accessible. Flour and sugar should be transferred into airtight containers after opening to prevent dampness and insect infestation.

You might want to store these items in a convenient basket placed on the counter near the stove.

Cutting Utensils

Knives should always be cleaned and dried after use. Place them in a safe place like a knife block well out of the reach of children.

The bottom of a ceramic bowl may be used to sharpen a knife if you have no grinding stone. Knives should be sharpened every two weeks.

Store the cutting board in a convenient location.

如何清理廚房

Cleaning Your Kitchen

It's important to form the good habit of cleaning your kitchen regularly. In this way grease never gets a chance to build up.

Countertops and Sinks

The countertop where food is prepared collects greasy dirt easily. Regular cleaning and maintenance are necessary.

Use liquid detergent on a washcloth to wash off the countertop, then rinse with water. If there is a heavy buildup of grease, use a brush with a household cleanser. The surface of a cut radish, when rubbed with cleanser over a sink or countertop, is also highly effective.

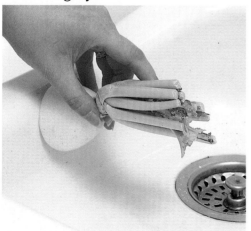

It's also very important to keep the kitchen drain flowing freely. There are many kinds of drain cleaners on the market. Follow directions for use at least once a month, and the drainpipe will remain unclogged.

Kitchen Fan

Regular cleaning of the kitchen exhaust fan is imperative. Take the fan apart and clean with a household cleanser.

In order to keep the stove top clean during this process, cover it first with a sheet of newspaper so grease and dirt don't fall onto the surface.

arbage

eat and leftovers can create very unpleasant
lors in your kitchen so you should have a
rbage can with a lid, lined with a plastic bag.
 avoid breakage, thick or double bags are
:st. Some garbage, such as fish and moist
od, should first be put into a plastic bag and
aled even before being placed in the garbage
n. Used tea leaves may be added to the can
 help dispel odors.

In order to keep your kitchen clean and sanitary, garbage should be removed every day, and the garbage can should be kept dry.

Place a sheet of newspaper on the stove

Dis-assemble the exhaust fan

Wash the fan parts

Clean the fan exterior

Refrigerator

Unless cleaned regularly, the refrigerator can easily be a source of odors.

However, rather than having to clean the refrigerator all the time, it is wise to carefully prepare the food that will be stored there. Use plastic wrap to cover meat, vegetables and leftovers; be sure that liquids like sodas and soy sauce are stored so they don't leak or spill. If such precautions aren't effective and bad odors prevail, lemons, apples, baking soda or fresheners can usually absorb other unpleasant odors.

Cover all leftovers for storage.

You may want to place clean paper on the shelves of the refrigerator so that they are easily replaced when dirty. This minimizes the number of times you will have to do a thorough cleaning.

Wipe the refrigerator with a diluted alcohol solution.

Should these things not work, however, a thorough cleaning is required. Empty the refrigerator, wipe the inner walls with a wet rag and then wipe again after spraying with a diluted alcohol solution (70% alcohol and 30% water). Finally, wash the door and the outside of the unit. Do not use household cleansers or hot water.

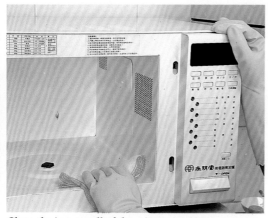

Clean the inner wall of the microwave oven.

Scrub the rack.

Oven and Microvawe

To clean the microwave, first remove the turntable and wash it. Then wipe the inner walls with a diluted cleanser followed by a clean, damp cloth. If material sticks to the walls, try bringing a bowl of water to a boil in the microwave so the steam created can help soften it, making it easier to remove.

Heat vinegar and water to deodorize the oven.

If you do not have a self-cleaning oven, wipe down the oven walls each time after use with a washcloth and a diluted cleanser while it is still warm; then wipe it again with a clean, damp cloth. Racks should be removed and cleaned when they have cooled off. If this is not done often, material becomes baked on and difficult to remove. The door of the oven should also be regularly removed, scrubbed on both sides with a hard brush, and replaced. Water and vinegar can be heated in your oven or microwave to absorb bad odors.

Gas Stove

Like the oven, the gas stove is easiest to clean while still warm. Remove the burner plates and their sealers and soak them in a solution of soapy water overnight, then scrub them with a scouring pad.

Clean the burner spill plate.

Clean the gas ring underneath the burner plate.

You can keep your burners from getting dirty by lining their spill plates with aluminum foil and periodically changing the foil when necessary. This can also be done to walls around the stove to prevent their ruin due to grease and oil spattering.

Cooking Utensils

If a kitchen knife becomes rusty, and you cannot remove the rust, throw the knife away. The rust will affect your food and your health. Rust may be removed with crushed white radish and cleanser applied with a scouring pad. After the rust is removed and the knife is completely dry it can be put away.

Cutting boards need to be cleaned after each use with a scouring pad, cleanser and, preferably, hot water.

A scorched metal pot is difficult to clean and can be easily damaged if scrubbed too vigorously with cleanser and a hard brush. Instead, it is better to boil lemon slices and water in the pot for five minutes. Let it sit for an hour, then scrub lightly. For enamel or porcelain pots, fill with hot water and a bit of sodium bicarbonate and soak for an hour. For cast iron, scrub the scorched area, heat the pot and then scrub with hot water and cleanser.

Boil lemon slices in your metal pots.

Clean enamel pots with hot water and sodium bicarbonate.

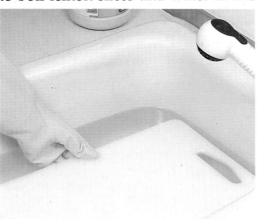

Disinfect the cutting board by soaking it in diluted bleach.

Cutting boards should also be bleached once a month. To do this, soak the board in a diluted bleach solution for about 30 minutes, and then rinse with water. You can use an old toothbrush with bleach to clean the knife marks.

Hang wash cloths to dry.

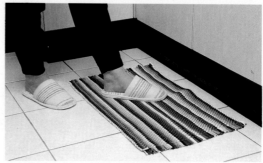
Kitchen mat to help keep floor dry.

Wash Cloths

Your wash rags can be washed with soap or, cleanser, rung out, and then hung to dry. Do not leave in the sink or they will become moldy. Every two or three days, soak your wash cloths in a diluted bleach solution overnight to disinfect them. Clean and dry all wash cloths and brushes after use. Should the cloths become too soiled or thread-bare, throw them away.

Keep sponges in a soap dish.

For sanitary purposes, washcloths should be categorized by their different uses: one for washing bowls, one for washing cooking utensils and one for drying off bowls and plates. Sponges and scrub brushes should also be cleaned and dried after use. Do not soak them in water as this could cause them to mold.

Kitchen Floor

It is inevitable that water or oil will be splashed onto the floor while you are cooking. Floors must be kept clean or they will attract insects and other pests. Sweeping, mopping with cleanser and rinsing should be performed two or three times a week.
Mats or area rugs on the kitchen floor should be kept clean and dry.

Kitchen Windows

Kitchen windows and window screens should be cleaned at least once a month. Remove the screens and scrub off greasy dirt after spraying with cleanser. The screen should be placed on news-paper to avoid a mess. Rinse with clean water, wash the windows themselves, then replace the screens.

Ingredients

2 whole chicken legs

1 T. preserved salted black beans

1 T. oyster sauce

1 T. chopped onion

3 stalks green onion, chopped

1 T. ginger root, minced

2 T. soy sauce

1/2 t. salt

1 T. cooking wine

1 C. oil

Instructions:

1. Soak black beans in water for 15 minutes; cu
chicken legs into bite-sized pieces. Add soy sauce
cooking wine, onions and chopped ginger to chicke
and allow the mixture to marinate.

2. Heat oil. Add chicken pieces, several at a tim
and deep fry for 5 minutes. Remove from oil

3. In another pan, bring 1 C. water, drained blac
beans, chicken marinade and oyster sauce to boi
Add chicken pieces and simmer on medium hea
for about 20 minutes. Remove chicken, evaporat
some of the sauce by cooking over high heat, ad
chopped green onions and then pour over chicke
to serve.

Ingredients

1 lb. shelled shrimp

1 lb. broccoli, cut into small florets

1 T. green onion, chopped

1 t. ginger root, minced

1/2 t. salt

1 T. cooking wine

1 T. cornstarch

4 T. oil

Instructions:

1. Slit the backs of the shrimp so they will become circular when cooked. Mix ginger, green onion, cooking wine and cornstarch together with shelled shrimp.

2. Heat 3 T. oil. Stir-fry shrimp over high heat until almost cooked through. Remove from oil.

3. Add 1 more T. oil and stir-fry broccoli over high heat for 1 minute to retain bright green color. Add 1/4 to 1/2 C. water, allow to simmer briefly and then add shrimp. Season with salt.

Ingredients

6 oz. ground meat (pork, beef, turkey, etc.)

1 10 oz. package frozen peas & carrots (thawed)

1/2 10 oz. package frozen corn (thawed)

4 eggs

1 T. green onion, chopped

1/2 T. soy sauce

1 t. salt

2 T. oil

Instructions:

1. Add soy sauce to ground meat, mix. Beat eggs, add green onion and 1-2 T. water.
2. Heat oil. When hot, add meat and fry until color changes. Add vegetables and mix well. Finally, add egg and cook, stirring, until egg is done. Season with salt.

Ingredients

2 cakes bean curd

6 oz. white meat fish, boned

2 stalks celery

1 t. ginger root, chopped

1 1/2 t. salt

1/2 T. cooking wine

Sesame oil, few drops

2 T. cornstarch

Instructions:

1. Cut bean curd into small pieces. Chop celery. Grind fish into paste, using food processor or mortar and pestle. Add chopped ginger root to fish paste and mix well.

2. Bring 5 C. of water to boil. Add bean curd and fish paste to cook for about 5 minutes, stirring to separate the fish particles. Add chopped celery and season mixture with salt and cooking wine. Mix the cornstarch with a small amount of cold water, then add to fish/bean curd to thicken. Sprinkle with a few drops of sesame oil and serve hot.

Ingredients

10 oz. pork, boneless

6 oz. soybean milk skin (usually available dried--must be soaked in tepid water before using)

1-2 carrots

1 t. ginger root, chopped

1 T. onion, chopped

1 t. salt

1 t. sugar

1/2 T. cornstarch

2 T. soy sauce

3 T. oil

1/2 T. cooking wine

Instructions

1. Shred pork and soybean milk skin. Cut carrot into strips, parboil and drain.
2. Mix together ginger, onion, cornstarch, wine and soy sauce.
3. Heat oil in pan. When hot, add pork and stir-fry until it loses color. Add carrot strips and soybean milk strips, stir-fry to mix evenly and then add ginger/soy sauce mixture. Stir, then add salt and sugar.

Ingredients

3 small pan size fish (pom-pano, etc.)

2-3 stalks green onion, cut into 2 inch pieces

3 slices ginger root

3 cloves garlic

1/2 t. salt

1 t. sugar

2 T. soy sauce

1 T. cooking wine

1/2 C. oil

Instructions:

1. Mix together ginger, cooking wine and soy sauce and let stand for a few minutes.
2. Heat oil in pan, add ginger slices and garlic cloves and sauté briefly. Add fish, fry on both sides. Pour in other seasonings together with salt and sugar. Cover pan and simmer for about 3 minutes until gravy thickens. Add green onions and serve.

Ingredients

8 dried mushrooms

1 can button mushrooms

10 oz. baby bok choy

1/2 t. salt

2 T. oyster sauce

1 T. cornstarch

2 T. oil

1 t. sugar

Instructions:

1. Soak dried mushrooms in warm water, then cut off stems. Parboil baby bok choy, arrange on dish.
2. Heat oil; stir-fry dried mushrooms and add canned mushrooms. Mix evenly. Add 2 C. water and oyster sauce; bring to boil. As mixture thickens, add salt and sugar. Mix cornstarch with small amounts of water to dissolve and add to mixture to thicken. Arrange mushrooms on plate as shown, pour sauce over and serve hot.

Ingredients

6 oz. pork fillet

3 oz. dried lily flowers

6 oz. small clams in shell

6 oz. quail eggs, hard boiled

3 green onions, cut into 2" pieces

1 1/2 t. salt

Few drops sesame oil

Instructions:

1. Soak dried lily flowers in warm water until softened. Shred pork.
2. Bring 5 C. water to boil, add lily flowers, quail eggs and scallions. Then add shredded pork and clams, cook for about 5 minutes over medium high heat. Season with salt. Sprinkle with sesame oil and serve hot.

Ingredients

1 lb. beef

8 oz. tender cabbage (inner leaves of nappa, bok choy, etc.)

1 T. onion, chopped

1 t. ginger root, chopped

1 small hot pepper, minced

2 T. soy sauce

1 t. salt

1 T. cornstarch

1/2 T. cooking wine

5 T. oil

Instructions:

1. Shred beef; add onion, ginger, pepper, soy sauce, 1/2 t. salt, cornstarch and cooking wine. Mix evenly and allow to stand.
2. Heat 2 T. oil in pan; stir-fry cabbage until cooked but still crunchy, add 1/2 t. salt for seasoning. Arrange on serving platter as bed for beef.
3. Heat 3 T. oil; add beef and stir-fry until color changes. Arrange on platter with cabbage and serve.
*Note: Do not overcook beef.

Ingredients

1 lb. squid

8 oz. lettuce

1 T. onion, chopped

1 t. ginger root, chopped

1 t. garlic, minced

1/2 T. red pepper, minced

1 T. soy sauce

1 T. tomato sauce

1/2 T. vinegar

Few drops sesame oil

Instructions:

1. Wash lettuce, then shred. Arrange on serving dish.
2. Mix together onion, ginger, red pepper, soy sauce, tomato sauce, vinegar and sesame oil. Let stand for flavors to mingle.
3. Wash squid, lean, and cut into cubes. Parboil, then drain, cool, and arrange on lettuce.
4. Pour seasoning mixture over squid evenly and serve.

Ingredients

3 blocks bean curd, cut into pieces

3 oz. snow peas

4 dried mushrooms

1 carrot

3 oz. bamboo shoot

1 T. onion, chopped

1 t. salt

1 t. sugar

1 T. cornstarch

2 T. soy sauce

Few drops sesame oil

Pepper to taste

Instructions:

1. Slice carrot and bamboo shoot into thin pieces. Soak dried mushrooms until soft; remove stems. Dice into pieces.
2. Bring 3 C. water to boil, add bean curd, mushrooms, carrots, bamboo shoots, soy sauce, salt, and sugar. Simmer for 15 minutes. Add snow peas to cook briefly. Mix cornstarch with small amount of water to dissolve; add to mixture to thicken. Add pepper, chopped onion and sesame oil to taste; serve hot.

Ingredients

1 lb. spareribs, chopped into 1" pieces

10 oz. taro

2 slices ginger root

3 stalks green onion, cut into 1" sections

1 t. onion, chopped

2 t. salt

1/2 T. cooking wine

Instructions:

1. Peel taro and dice. Parboil ribs, drain.
2. Bring 5 C. water to a boil; add spareribs, ginger and green onion. Simmer for 15 minutes. Remove ginger and green onion slices. Add taro and cook over medium heat for 15 minutes. Add cooking wine and salt. Add chopped onion and serve hot.
*Note: If green onion and ginger are left in soup for too long, they impart a bitterness to the broth.

Ingredients

1 lb. spareribs, cut into 1" pieces

6 oz. pineapple

1 green pepper

1 t. ginger chopped

1 T. onion chopped

1/2 t. salt

3 T. tomato sauce

1 C. flour

2 T. soy sauce

1 T. cooking wine

Instructions:

1. Cut pineapple and green pepper into chunks.
2. Mix together soy sauce, ginger, salt and cooking wine. Add ribs and marinate for a few minutes. Dust ribs with flour.
3. Heat 2 C. oil. When hot, add ribs and cook over high heat for 1-2 minutes. Lower heat and continue to fry for about 5 minutes longer. Remove ribs from oil. Re-heat oil and add ribs, frying again for 1 minute. Remove from oil and drain.
4. Remove oil from pan, save about 3 T. Stir-fry green pepper and remove. Add tomato sauce and spareribs; mix well and fry together. Add green pepper, pineapple chunks and chopped onion. Mix well and serve hot.

Ingredients

1 lb. fresh shrimp, shelled

5 cloves of garlic

1 t. ginger root, chopped

1 T. green onion, chopped

1 t. salt

1 T. soy sauce

1/2 T. cooking wine

1 T. oil

Instructions:

1. Mix shrimp with wine, salt and ginger. Arrange on steam proof plate.
2. Heat oil, stir-fry chopped garlic. Remove garlic and mix with soy sauce; pour over shrimp mixture evenly. Steam platter over high heat for 3 minutes until shrimp is done. Sprinkle with chopped green onion and serve hot.

Ingredients:

1 lb. mustard greens

2 dried scallops

1 t. salt

1/2 t. sugar

1/2 T. soy sauce

2 T. oil

Few drops sesame oil

Instructions:

1. Wash and slice mustard greens. Boil scallops until tender. Shred scallops into thin strips.
2. Parboil mustard greens and drain.
3. Heat oil and stir-fry mustard greens. Add 1 C. water and scallops, simmer briefly. Add salt, sugar, and soy sauce. Finally, thicken with cornstarch solution and sprinkle with sesame oil. Serve hot.

Ingredients:

1 lb. winter melon

8 oz. mussels, shelled

Several ginger slices

3 stalks green onion in 1" sections

1 1/2 t. salt

1/2 T. cooking wine

Several drops sesame oil

Instructions:

1. Peel and dice winter melon.
2. Bring 5 C. water to boil; add winter melon, ginger slices, green onion and mussels. Bring to boil again then lower heat and simmer until winter melon is tender. Add salt and cooking wine for seasoning. Sprinkle with sesame oil and serve hot.

Ingredients:

1 lb. white meat fish (halibut, cod, etc.)

1 onion

1 carrot

3 stalks green onion, cut into 1" sections

1 t. ginger root, chopped

1 t. garlic, chopped

2 T. fermented bean paste

1 T. soy sauce

1/2 t. salt

1 t. sugar

1 T. cooking wine

1/2 C. oil

Instructions:

1. Slice fish, add salt, ginger and cooking wine to marinate for a few minutes. Slice onion and carrot.
2. Heat oil and fry fish slices until golden brown. Arrange on plate. Heat 2 T. oil and stir-fry green onion, onion and garlic. Add fermented bean paste, soy sauce and sugar, stir-fry and mix evenly. Add fish, carrot, and small amounts of water. Simmer for 5 minutes until sauce is absorbed.

Ingredients:

1 lb. green vegetable stems
(broccoli stems)

1 lb. pork filet

1 t. ginger root, chopped

1 T. red pepper paste

1 T. soy sauce

1 t. sugar

1/2 T. cooking wine

1 T. cornstarch

3 T. oil

Instructions:

1. Peel stems and cut into thick slices. Slice pork into thin strips; add ginger, wine, cornstarch and soy sauce and mix thoroughly.
2. Heat oil; add pork and stir-fry. When pork is partially done, add vegetable stems and continue to stir-fry until done. Season with red pepper paste and sugar. Serve hot.

Ingredients:

1 lb. tender greens (tender pea leaves, spinach, etc.)

6 oz. crab meat

1 egg white

1/2 t. sugar

1 t. salt

1 T. cornstarch

3 T. oil

Instructions:

1. Remove any hard stems of greens.
2. Heat oil and stir-fry greens; add salt for seasoning, then remove. Place on serving dish.
3. Bring 1 C. water to a boil, add crab meat, season with 1/2 t. salt and sugar, and add egg white. Thicken with cornstarch solution and pour over greens.

* Note: Fresh crab meat will taste better than imitation or canned.

Ingredients:

10 oz. ground pork

1 large cucumber, peeled and seeded

3 stalks green onion in 1" pieces

1 t. ginger root, chopped

1 T. cooking wine

1 T. cornstarch

1 egg white

1 1/2 t. salt

Instructions:

1. Slice cucumber. Add ginger, 1/2 t. salt, wine, egg white and cornstarch to ground pork, mix evenly and make into small meatballs.
2. Bring 5 C. water to a boil; add meatballs to cook. Add cucumber and green onion; cook until cucumber is tender. Add 1 t. salt for seasoning. Serve hot.

Ingredients:

10 oz. beef or pork jerky

4 stalks scallions, cut in 1" sections

1/2 T. cooking wine

1/4 t. salt

2 T. oil

Instructions:

1. Heat oil, stir-fry jerky for 1 minute. Add scallions and stir-fry briefly. Add wine and salt. Serve hot.
* Note: Do not add too much salt since jerky is already salted. If you like scallions, you may increase amount as desired.

Ingredients:

1 lb. eggplant

3 oz. ground pork

1 T. chopped edible fungus

1 T. water chestnuts, chopped

2 T. green onion, chopped

1 T. garlic, chopped

1 T. hot fermented bean paste

1 T. soy sauce

4 T. oil

1/2 t. vinegar

1/2 t. cornstarch

1 t. sugar

1/2 t. salt

Instructions:

1. Slice eggplants (if Western eggplant, remove skin) in 1 1/2" thickness. Heat 3 T. oil and fry eggplant until well done. Remove and drain.

2. Heat 1 T. oil; fry pork. Add bean paste, garlic, soy sauce, salt, vinegar and sugar. Then add fungus, water chestnuts, and eggplant; cook for 3 minutes. Finally, thicken with cornstarch solution and sprinkle with green onion. Serve hot.

Ingredients:

3 cubes bean curd, each cut into 4 triangular pieces

3 oz. ground pork

3 oz. shrimp

Small amount of greens (alfalfa sprouts, etc.)

1 t. ginger root, chopped

1 egg

1/2 t. cooking wine

1 t. salt

1 t. sugar

1 T. soy sauce

1/2 T. cornstarch

1 C. oil

Instructions:

1. Mince shrimp and add to pork together with 1/2 t. salt, wine, egg yolk and 1/2 T. cornstarch.

2. Make a small hole in one side of each piece of bean curd, dust with cornstarch and fill with pork mixture.

3. Heat oil. Fry bean curd, filled side down. Remove and drain. Remove oil from pan, leaving 1 T. Add 1 C. water, soy sauce, 1/2 t. salt and sugar. Place soy bean cakes in pan and cover to simmer 10 minutes. Add greens to cook for 1/2 minute. Thicken with cornstarch solution and serve hot.

Ingredients:

1 lb. spareribs, cut in 1" pieces

10 oz. seaweed, tied into knots

3 slices ginger root

1 stalk green onion

1 T. cooking wine

1 1/2 t. salt

Instructions:

1. Parboil spareribs for 10 minutes and remove. Rinse and drain. Place in pot and add 5 C. water, green onion and ginger. Bring to boil, then lower to simmer. Add seaweed knots and cooking wine. Simmer for about 40 minutes; season with salt. Serve hot.

Ingredients:

1 lb. beef tenderloin

4 stalks green onion

1 red pepper

1 T. cooking wine

2 T. soy sauce

1 t. salt

1 t. sugar

1 T. cornstarch

5 T. oil

Instructions:

1. Slice beef thinly; add salt, soy sauce, sugar, ginger, wine and cornstarch and mix evenly. Allow to marinate for 10 minutes.
2. Slice green onion at a slant into 1" pieces.
3. Heat oil. Stir-fry beef until medium rare. Remove.
4. Remove all but 2 T. oil. Fry green onion and red pepper; add beef to mingle flavors. Serve hot.

Ingredients:

10 oz. lean pork

6 oz. pumpkin (like kabocha)

6 oz. cucumber

1 T. chopped green onion

1 t. salt

2 t. soy sauce

1/2 T. cooking wine

1/2 T. cornstarch

4 T. oil

Instructions:

1. Cut pork into 1/2" cubes. Add soy sauce, wine and cornstarch; mix by hand. Marinate for about 10 minutes.

2. Remove pumpkin skin and seeds if any; cut into 1/2" cubes. Cut cucumber into 1/2" cubes also.

3. Heat oil. When moderately hot, add pumpkin and fry for about 1 minute. Remove.

4. Remove half of oil from pan: heat remainder again. When hot, add pork and fry at high heat until almost done. Add pumpkin and cucumber, salt, and green onion. Stir to mix evenly. Serve hot.

Ingredients:

10 oz. squid, cleaned and skinned

8 oz. celery

1 T. green onion, chopped

1 t. ginger, chopped

1 T. soy sauce

1 1/2 t. salt

3 T. oil

1 T. cooking wine

Instructions:

1. Cut diamond pattern into squid; slice squid into diagonal pieces, 1/2" wide and 2" long. Parboil until white.
2. Slice celery diagonally into 1/2" width pieces.
3. Heat oil. When hot, add ginger. After oil is fragrant, add celery together with wine soy sauce and salt.
4. Add squid and continue to stir-fry until celery is crisp and tender. Sprinkle with green onion and serve hot.

Ingredients:

2 tomatoes

6 oz. bean sprouts

1 T. green onion, chopped

1 1/2 t. salt

1 t. sesame oil

Instructions:

1. Cut tomatoes into bite-sized pieces. Remove roots of bean sprouts and rinse clean.
2. Place tomatoes and bean sprouts in 5 C. water; bring to boil and then simmer over medium heat for 10 minutes. Add salt. Sprinkle with green onion and sesame oil. Serve hot.

Ingredients:

1 1/2 lb. spareribs, chopped into 1" pieces

6 oz. pineapple chunks

1 t. garlic, chopped

1 T. cooking wine

1 T. soy sauce

2 T. tomato sauce

1/2 T. salt

1 t. sugar

4 T. cornstarch

2 C. oil

1/2 T. vinegar

Instructions:

1. Mix 1/2 t. salt together with soy sauce, wine and garlic; add to ribs, stir to coat and marinate for 20 minutes. Dust with cornstarch.
2. Heat oil. When hot, deep fry ribs over moderate heat. As ribs become browned, remove and drain. Reheat oil and fry ribs once again for 1 minute. Remove.
3. In a pan, heat 2 T. of frying oil. Add tomato sauce, sugar and vinegar and bring mixture to a boil.
4. Add ribs and pineapple and braise until sauce is fully absorbed. May be garnished with preserved sweet and sour cucumber.

Ingredients:

10 oz. large shrimp, cleaned and shelled

10 oz. pork kidney

6 oz. Chinese cabbage or spinach

1 T. green onion, chopped

2. t. ginger, chopped

1 t. garlic, chopped

1 T. cooking wine

1 T. soy sauce

1 1/2 t. salt

1 T. cornstarch

4 T. oil

Instructions:

1. Mix 1/2 t. wine, 1 t. ginger, and 1/2 T. cornstarch and add to shrimp.

2. Cut kidney in half; score the surface in squares. Slice in diagonal strips. Add 1/2 T. wine, soy sauce, 1 t. ginger, garlic and 1/2 T. cornstarch; mix evenly.

3. Heat 2 T. oil and stir-fry vegetables over high heat for 1 minute; season with 1/2 t. salt. Remove from pan and place on serving platter.

4. Heat 2 t. oil in pan; add shrimp and stir-fry quickly. Add kidney slices, green onions and 1 t. salt. Stir-fry until kidney is tender and done. Remove, pour over vegetables and serve hot.

Ingredients:

10 oz. winter vegetable (salted preserved mustard greens)

6 oz. dried bean curd cubes, cut into small pieces

1 red pepper

1/2 t. salt

1 t. sugar

1 T. soy sauce

1 T. green onion, chopped

3 T. oil

Instructions:

1. Rinse winter vegetable, squeeze dry, then shred each leaf.
2. Heat oil. When hot, add dried bean curd and stir-fry for 30 seconds.
3. Add winter vegetable shreds, green onion, and sliced red pepper and continue to stir-fry. Season with salt, sugar, and soy sauce and cook until done.

Ingredients:

1 1/2 lb. winter melon

3 oz. dried shrimp

1 sheet dried seaweed

Ginger root, 3-4 slices

1 stalk green onion, cut into 1" lengths

1/2 T. cooking wine

1 1/2 t. salt

1 t. sesame oil

Instructions:

1. Peel winter melon and remove seeds. Cut into bite-sized pieces. Soak dried shrimp in hot water.
2. Put winter melon in pot with 4 C. water; bring to boil over high heat. Reduce heat.
3. Add dried shrimp, ginger slices, green onions and wine; cook for about 15 minutes.
4. Add salt. Tear seaweed into small pieces and sprinkle over soup. Add sesame oil and serve.

Ingredients:

10 oz. pork belly

5 dried mushrooms (like shiitake)

6 oz. preserved winter vegetable
(salted, preserved mustard greens)

1 T. cooking wine

1 T. soy sauce

1 stalk green onion, cut in 1" lengths

2 C. oil

Instructions:

1. Slice pork belly into thin pieces, 3" x 2". Add soy sauce, wine and green onion, mix well and marinate for 20 minutes.
2. Soak mushrooms in cold water to soften; remove stems. Rinse preserved winter vegetable twice.
3. Heat oil; when hot, reduce heat to medium. Deep-fry pork until golden; remove.
4. Arrange mushrooms, cap down, in middle of a steam proof bowl with pork strips along both sides. Cover with preserved winter vegetable.
5. Bring water in steamer to boil. Place bowl over steam, cover and steam over low heat for 1 hour.
6. Remove and turn contents of bowl upside down into serving platter. Serve hot.

Ingredients:

4 oz. cashews, unsalted

10 oz. boned chicken breast

1/2 t. cooking wine

1 t. salt

1 t. sugar

1/2 T. soy sauce

1 T. cornstarch

3 T. oil

Instructions:

1. Cut chicken into small cubes. Add salt, sugar, soy sauce, wine and cornstarch; mix evenly and marinate for 10 minutes.

2. Heat 3 T. oil. When oil is hot, reduce heat to medium and fry cashews for 30 seconds. Remove.

3. Reheat oil and stir fry chicken over high heat until almost done. Add cashew nuts, stir and serve hot.

Ingredients:

10 oz. cabbage

1 green onion

1 1/2 T. vinegar

1 t. sugar

1/2 T. cornstarch

3 T. oil

1 t. salt

Instructions:

1. Wash cabbage and cut into bite-size pieces.
2. Heat 3 T. oil in the pan. When hot, fry cabbage and diced green onion at high heat for three minutes; add salt to season. Lower to medium heat, add a small amount of water and simmer for about 3 minutes. Remove from heat.
3. Add sugar and vinegar to the marinade for more flavor. Thicken with cornstarch/water mixture. Finally, add the cooked cabbage and mix evenly. Serve hot.

Ingredients:

10 oz. ground pork

1 Chinese cabbage

1 bundle dried bean flour noodles

1 t. ginger root, chopped

1 T. chopped green onion

2 t. salt

1/2 T. cornstarch

1/2 T. cooking wine

Instructions:

1. Select large Chinese cabbage leaves. Soak in hot water for 10 seconds to soften. Soak bean flour noodles in hot water to soften.
2. Add green onion, ginger, cornstarch, wine and sugar to ground pork to make meat filling.
3. Place some meat filling on a cabbage leaf and roll. Seal ends with cornstarch to prevent filling from escaping during cooking.
4. Bring 5 C. water to boil. Lay stuffed leaves in water; lower heat to medium and cook for 15 minutes. Add 1 t. salt for seasoning.
5. Add drained, softened bean flour noodles and cook for an additional minute. Serve hot.

Ingredients:

8 oz. shrimp, shelled and cleaned

8 oz. cod

10 oz. ground pork

5 pieces soy milk skin

1 t. ginger root

1 T. chopped green onion

2 T. powdered milk

1 t. sugar

1 t. salt

1 T. cornstarch

1 T. cooking wine

2 C. oil

Instructions:

1. Use a food processor and mince shrimp. Grind cod in processor as well. Cut soy milk skin into rectangles.

2. Mix shrimp, cod and ground pork together with ginger, onion, milk powder, salt, sugar, cornstarch, wine and a small amount of water to make filling.

3. Place filling onto soy milk skins and roll into egg roll-like shape.

4. Heat oil. When hot, fry rolls over low heat for 5 minutes. Remove from oil.

5. Reheat oil. When hot, add rolls and fry once again until golden and crispy.

Ingredients:

8 oz. sea cucumber

8 oz. ground pork

6 oz. carrot

6 oz. bamboo shoots

6 oz. mushrooms

1 egg white

1 t. ginger root, chopped

3 stalks green onion, cut into 1" pieces

1 t. salt

2 T. soy sauce

1 t. sugar

1/2 T. cooking wine

1 T. cornstarch

Instructions:

1. Cut sea cucumber into bite-sized cubes. Slice carrot and bamboo shoots into thin slices.

2. Mix 1/2 t. salt together with ginger, cornstarch, egg white and wine; add to ground pork, mix evenly and make small meatballs.

3. Bring 3 C. water to boil. Add meatball then sea cucumber, carrots, bamboo shoots, mushrooms, green onions and soy sauce. Simmer until sea cucumber is tender. Season with salt, sugar and wine. Simmer until gravy is absorbed.

4. Thicken with cornstarch/water solution; serve hot.

Ingredients:

8 oz. dried bean curd noodle

8 oz. celery

1 T. chopped green onion

1/2 T. chopped hot pepper

3 T. soy sauce

1 T. sugar

Sesame oil

1 T. vinegar

Instructions:

1. Dip noodles into boiling water, remove and drain.
2. Slice celery into strips.
3. Dilute sugar with a small amount of warm water; add chopped green onion, hot pepper, soy sauce, vinegar and a few drops of sesame oil. Mix thoroughly.
4. Arrange celery strips on plate. Add noodles and, finally, salad dressing.

Ingredients:

10 oz. lotus root

10 oz. chicken

3 stalks green onion, sliced in 2"
pieces

3 slices ginger

1 1/2 t. salt

1 T. cooking wine

Instructions:

1. Cut lotus root and chicken into bite-sized pieces.
Dip into boiling water for short time and remove.
2. Place lotus root, chicken, green onion and ginger
in 5 C. water; bring to boil. Reduce heat and simmer
for 20 minutes.
3. Season with salt and wine; serve hot.

Ingredients:

8 oz. chives

10 oz. pork liver

1 T. chopped green onion

1 t. ginger, chopped

2 T. soy sauce

1/2 t. salt

1 t. sugar

1 T. cooking wine

1 T. cornstarch

4 T. oil

Instructions:

1. Cut chives into 1" lengths; slice liver into thin pieces.
2. Mix onion, ginger, soy sauce, wine and cornstarch with liver.
3. Heat 2 T. oil. When hot, stir-fry chives over high heat until soft. Remove and place onto plate.
4. Add 2 more T. oil, heat and stir-fry liver over high heat until color changes. Add chives to mix evenly, season with salt and sugar. Serve hot.

Ingredients:

10 oz. lima beans, shelled

10 oz. lean pork

1 t. ginger, chopped

2 T. soy sauce

1 t. salt

1 T. cornstarch

1 T. cooking wine

4 T. oil

Instructions:

1. Slice pork thinly; add soy sauce, ginger, cornstarch and wine. Mix together and allow to marinate.
2. Heat 3 T. oil. When hot, stir-fry meat over high heat until almost done. Remove.
3. Add 1 T. oil to pan. When hot, stir-fry lima beans and then add a small amount of water and allow to simmer until beans are tender.
4. Add meat, mix thoroughly and season with salt. Serve hot.

Ingredients:

6 oz. bacon strips

10 oz. lettuce

1/2 t. salt

3 T. oil

Instructions:

1. Cut lettuce and bacon into bite-sized pieces.
2. Heat pan and fry bacon until crisp. Remove.
3. Add oil to pan. When hot, stir-fry lettuce until crisp and tender; add bacon to mix evenly. Season with salt. Serve hot.

Ingredients:

8 oz. turnips

1 whole white meat fish, cleaned & scaled

1 T. chopped green onion

3 stalks green onion, 2" slices

Shredded ginger root

1 1/2 t. salt

1 T. cooking wine

Few drops sesame oil

Instructions:

1. Cut turnip into strips.
2. Add turnip, ginger and green onion pieces to 5 C. water and bring to boil.
3. Add fish and simmer for 15 minutes; season with salt and wine.
4. Before serving sprinkle with sesame oil and chopped green onion.

Ingredients:

1 lb. salted dried duck

6 stalks scallion, shredded

3 red peppers, seeded and sliced in thin strips

1 t. sugar

1/2 T. cooking wine

1 t. sesame oil

Instructions:

1. If duck is not cooked, steam for 20 minutes remove and bone.
2. Slice duck meat thinly; add sugar, wine and sesame oil to mix evenly.
3. Mix with scallion and red pepper. Serve.

Ingredients:

1 lb. squid, skinned and cleaned

8 oz. cucumber

1 t. chopped ginger root

2 stalks green onion, 1" pieces

1 t. salt

1 hot red pepper

1/2 T. soy sauce

1/2 T. cooking wine

3 T. oil

1/2 T. cornstarch

Instructions:

1. Slice cucumber into thin diagonal pieces.
2. Score squid in diamond pattern; slice into bite-sized pieces. Parboil.
3. Heat oil. When hot stir-fry ginger, green onion and hot pepper slices. Add squid and cucumber, stir-fry evenly. Add soy sauce, salt and wine. Thicken with cornstarch/water solution. Serve hot.

Ingredients:

1 chicken leg

1 can sliced pineapple

1 t. salt

2 stalks green onion, 1" pieces

1 thin slice ginger

1/3 bundle agar agar

Instructions:

1. Parboil chicken; bone and cube meat. Add salt, green onion and ginger; allow to marinate.

2. Cut pineapple into bite-sized pieces. Place pineapple chunks, pineapple juice and chicken in pot; bring to boil.

3. Lower heat and add agar agar. After agar agar melts, pour mixture into deep boil.

4. Mixture gels as it cools. Turn over onto plate and remove from bowl. Serve garnished with greens.

Ingredients:

8 oz. bitter melon

8 oz. spareribs, cut into 1"
pieces

6 oz. prepared fishballs

3 stalks green onion, 1" pieces

2 thin slices ginger

1 1/2 t. salt

Few drops sesame oil

1/2 T. cooking wine

Instructions:

1. Remove seeds from bitter melon; slice into bite-sized pieces. Parboil spareribs.
2. Place ginger, green onion, bitter melon, spareribs and   fishballs in 5 C. water; bring to boil. Reduce heat and simmer for 20 minutes. Season with salt and wine.
3. Sprinkle with sesame oil and serve hot.

Ingredients:

10 oz. scallops

6 oz. broccoli

6 oz. canned mushrooms

6 oz. baby corn

1 t. chopped ginger

1 T. green onion

1 t. salt

1/2 T. soy sauce

1/2 T. cooking wine

1/2 T. cornstarch

3 T. oil

Instructions:

1. Cut baby corn into bite-sized pieces.
2. Bring 3 C. water to boil. Add scallops, broccoli, baby corn and parboil. Remove and drain.
3. Heat oil. When hot, stir-fry ginger. Add scallops, broccoli, baby corn and mushrooms. Stir-fry to mix evenly, season with soy sauce, salt and wine. Sprinkle with chopped green onion.
4. Thicken with cornstarch/water solution. Serve hot.

Jellied Pigs Feet

Ingredients:

1 1/2 lb. pigs feet

2 star anises

3 stalks green onion, 2" slices

3 ginger pieces, cut in 2" sections

1 t. salt

2 T. Shao Hsing wine

Instructions:

1. Clean pigs feet; cut into small cubes and parboil. Remove.

2. Place green onion, ginger, star anise and pigs feet in 5 C. water; bring to boil. Reduce heat and simmer for 20 minutes. Remove green onion, ginger, star anise; continue to simmer for 30 minutes. Add Shao Hsing wine and salt to season.

3. Allow mixture to cool; place in refrigerator for 1 hour. Serve cold.

Ingredients:

6 oz. mushrooms

8 oz. baby bok choy

1 t. salt

1 t. sugar

1/2 T. soy sauce

1/2 T. cornstarch

Few drops sesame oil

Instructions:

1. Remove mushroom stems; slice mushrooms diagonally. Cut baby bok choy in halves.

2. Bring 5 C. water to boil. Add mushrooms and bok choy to cook for 5 minutes. Remove water, save 1/2 cup.

3. Add soy sauce, salt and sugar to season; thicken with cornstarch/water mixture and sprinkle with sesame oil. Serve hot.

Ingredients:

1 lb. beef shank

6 oz. tomatoes

6 oz. carrots

6 oz. potatoes

3 stalks green onion, 2" slices

3 slices ginger

1 1/2 t. salt

1 T. cooking wine

1 T. chopped green onion

Instructions:

1. Peel potatoes and carrots; cut together with tomatoes into bite-sized pieces.
2. Parboil beef shank and remove. Cut into thick pieces.
3. Place green onion, ginger, beef and tomatoes in 5 C. water; bring to boil over high heat. Reduce heat and simmer for one hour. Add potatoes and carrots and simmer for 20 minutes longer.
4. Season with salt and wine. Sprinkle with green onion and serve hot.

Ingredients:

1 lb. boneless pork chops

6 oz. canned mushrooms

4 oz. carrots

1 C. flour

3 stalks green onion, 2" slices

1 t. chopped ginger

1/2 t. salt

1 t. sugar

3 T. soy sauce

1/2 T. cooking wine

2 T. oil

Instructions:

1. Slice mushrooms; cut carrot into strips.
2. Add green onion, ginger, soy sauce and wine to pork chops and allow to marinate briefly.
3. Dredge with flour, then deep fry in hot oil until golden brown.
4. Heat 2 T. oil in pan; when hot, stir-fry mushrooms and carrots. Add 2 C. water and marinade and bring to boil. Add pork chops and simmer for 20 minutes, season with salt and sugar.
5. Serve hot.

Ingredients:

10 oz. boneless chicken breast

8 oz. cucumbers

6 oz. carrots

2 T. red pepper oil

1 t. chopped garlic

1 T. chopped green onion

1 t. salt

Instructions:

1. Boil or steam chicken until cooked but still tender; tear into long strips. While still hot, add salt.

2. Slice cucumber and carrot into strips. Parboil briefly. Remove and drain; allow to cool.

3. Heat red pepper oil; fry chopped garlic. Remove from heat and cool.

4. Mix cooked chicken, cucumber, carrot, chopped green onion and red pepper oil together. Serve cold.

Ingredients:

1 1/2 lb. crab

1 bundle Chinese vermicelli

5 stalks green onion, 2" slices

2 t. chopped ginger

1/2 t. salt

2 t. sugar

3 T. soy sauce

2 T. Chinese barbecue sauce

Cornstarch

1 C. oil

Instructions:

1. Clean crab; cut into 1" pieces and dip in cornstarch.
2. Soak Chinese vermicelli until soft. Drain.
3. Mix ginger, sugar, soy sauce, and Chinese barbecue sauce. Reserve.
4. Heat 1 C. oil. When hot, deep fry crab pieces for about 2 minutes and remove.
5. Heat 2 T. oil in pan. When hot, fry green onion pieces and then add reserved seasoning mixture. Bring to boil and add crab pieces.
6. Place vermicelli together with 1 C. water in a porcelain cooking pot; bring to a boil and season with salt. Arrange crab pieces over and cover to simmer for 1 minute. Serve hot.

Ingredients:

2 small squirrelfish

2 red apples

3 stalks green onion, 1" pieces

1 T. chopped green onion

1 1/2 t. salt

Few drops sesame oil

1 T. cooking wine

Instructions:

1. Peel apple; cut into bite-sized cubes.
2. Place ginger, green onion and apple in 5 C. water; bring to boil. Reduce heat and simmer for 10 minutes. Add fish and simmer for 10 minutes more.
3. Season with salt and wine. Sprinkle with chopped green onion and sesame oil; serve hot.
* Note: This is a sweet and fragrant combination well worth trying!

Ingredients:

1 pig foot, cleaned and cut in small pieces

3 stalks green onion, cut in 2" pieces

1/2 t. chopped ginger

1/2 C. rock sugar

4 T. soy sauce

1 T. cooking wine

2 C. oil

Instructions:

1. Parboil pigs foot.
2. Mix green onion, ginger, salt, soy sauce, wine and rock sugar; add to pigs foot pieces and marinate for 1 1/2 hours.
3. Heat 2 C. oil. When hot, add pigs foot and deep-fry. Remove and drain.
4. Bring 5 C. water and marinade to boil over high heat. Add pigs foot pieces, reduce heat and simmer for 1 hour, allowing gravy to be absorbed.
*Note: Do not allow ingredients to dry out during simmering process. Add water as necessary.

Ingredients:

8 oz. ground pork

1 lb. large cucumber

3 dried mushrooms

6 oz. water chestnut

1 egg white

1 t. chopped ginger

1 T. chopped green onion

1 t. salt

1 1/2 t. soy sauce

1/2 T. cooking wine

1 1/2 T. cornstarch

Sesame oil

Instructions:

1. Peel cucumber, cut into 1" pieces crosswise. Scoop out seeds. Soak dried mushrooms until soft; chop. Mince water chestnuts.
2. Mix ground pork with ginger, green onions, mushrooms, water chestnuts, egg white, salt, cornstarch, 1 T. soy sauce, wine and a few drops of sesame oil. Mix together well.
3. Dust opening in cucumber pieces with cornstarch; fill with ground meat mixture and arrange in steamer. Steam for 15 minutes and then remove.
4. Pour juices from steam plate into pan; add small amount of water and 1/2 T. soy sauce and bring to boil. Thicken with cornstarch/water solution and pour over cucumber.

Ingredients:

1 lb. broccoli

1/2 C. milk

1 t. salt

1 T. cream

1 t. sugar

1 T. cornstarch

Instructions:

1. Wash and cut broccoli into small florets.
2. Bring 1/2 C. water, salt, sugar and milk to boil; add broccoli and simmer for 5 minutes.
3. Thicken with cornstarch/water solution. Add cream and serve hot.

Ingredients:

1 pork belly

8 oz. lotus seeds

6 oz. red dates

3 slices ginger

3 stalks green onion, 2" pieces

1 1/2 t. salt

1 T. cooking wine

Instructions:

1. Clean pork belly thoroughly; remove excess fat.
2. Cut 4" opening; turn inside out. Use mixture of 1 T. rock salt and 1 T. vinegar to scrub and remove any stickiness. Rinse clean with water. Put in boiling water to cook 3 minutes and remove. Scrape off any scum and rinse clean. Slice into pieces.
3. Bring 6 C. water together with pork, red dates, lotus seeds, green onion and ginger slices to boil. Reduce heat and simmer for 1 1/2 to 2 hours. Season with salt and wine and serve hot.

Ingredients:

Two chicken legs

3 cakes fried bean curd

2 slices ginger

3 stalks green onions, 1" pieces

1 T. chopped green onion

1/2 t. salt

1 t. sugar

1/2 T. cooking wine

3 t. soy sauce

1/2 C. oil

Instructions:

1. Chop the legs into 1" pieces. Add 1 T. soy sauce, ginger, green onion and wine; marinate chicken with this mixture.
2. Cut fried bean curd into 1 1/2" cubes.
3. Heat oil in pan. When hot, fry chicken pieces until lightly browned. Remove excess oil.
4. Add 3 C. water, fried bean curd and 2 T. soy sauce. Bring to boil over high heat.
5. Reduce heat and simmer for 20 minutes. Add salt and sugar to season.
6. Increase heat to evaporate some of the liquid. Sprinkle with chopped green onion and serve hot.

Ingredients:

1 lb. beef

10 oz. bean sprouts

1 t. chopped ginger

1 T. chopped green onion

1/2 t. salt

2 T. soy sauce

1 T. cornstarch

1 T. cooking wine

5 T. oil

Instructions:

1. Remove both ends of each bean sprout.
2. Shred beef; add soy sauce, wine, chopped green onion, ginger and cornstarch and mix well.
3. Heat 3 T. oil; when hot, stir-fry beef quickly until color changes. Remove.
4. Heat pan again with 2 T. oil. When hot, stir-fry bean sprouts and then add 1/2 C. water.
5. Add beef, season with salt and serve.

Ingredients:

10 oz. spinach

3 oz. bean curd skin

1 t. salt

Small amount of baking soda

3 T. oil

Instructions:

1. Slice bean curd skin into thin strips and soak in water with baking soda added. Rinse clean and parboil. Remove and drain.

2. Remove any hard stems from spinach.

3. Heat oil. When hot, stir-fry spinach for 1 minute. Add bean curd skin and stir-fry evenly. Season with salt.

*Note: Bean curd skin is as thin as parchment paper and not easy to work with. It cannot be cooked for too long. Hence, we recommend that it be soaked in soda water solution first so that it is softened before use.

Ingredients:

10 oz. lean boneless pork

10 oz. pickled cabbage

Shredded ginger

3 stalks green onion, 2" sections

1 t. salt

1 T. cooking wine

Sesame oil

Black pepper

Instructions:

1. Slice pork into thin slices; cut pickled cabbage into bite-sized cubes.
2. Place cabbage, ginger and green onion in 5 C. water; bring to boil. Reduce heat and cook for 10 minutes.
3. After sourness of cabbage has dissipated, add pork. When pork is done, add salt and wine. Sprinkle with sesame oil and pepper and serve hot.

Ingredients:

1 lb. duck's feet

8 oz. cucumber

1 hot red pepper, cut in strips

1/2 T. chopped garlic

1 t. chopped ginger

1/2 t. salt

1 t. sugar

1 T. hot pepper paste

1/2 T. vinegar

Sesame oil

Instructions:

1. Parboil duck feet; de-bone and dip in ice water. Change water three times.
2. Remove cucumber ends and cut into strips.
3. Mix red pepper, cucumber, salt, sugar, vinegar, sesame oil, hot pepper paste, garlic and ginger thoroughly. Add to duck feet and marinate for 30 minutes.
4. Arrange on platter and serve cold.

Ingredients:

8 oz. pork belly

13 oz. kelp tied in knots

3 ginger slices

3 stalks green onion, 1" pieces

1/2 t. salt

1 t. sugar

2 1/2 T. soy sauce

1/2 T. cooking wine

1/2 C. oil

Instructions:

1. Slice pork belly into bite-size pieces; add 1/2 T. soy sauce and mix evenly. Stir-fry in hot pan until lightly browned; remove.
2. Bring 2 C. water, pork, kelp, ginger, green onion and 2 T. soy sauce to boil. Reduce heat and simmer for 30 minutes until kelp is tender.
3. Season with salt, sugar and wine. Cook at high heat to reduce gravy. Serve hot.

Ingredients:

1 lb. ground pork

1 salted preserved egg

3 dried mushrooms

1 egg white

1 T. chopped green onion

1 t. chopped ginger

1/2 t. salt

1 t. sesame oil

1 t. sugar

1 T. cornstarch

1 1/2 T. soy sauce

1/2 T. cooking wine

Instructions:

1. Remove yolk from salted egg. Mince egg white. Soak dried mushrooms until soft; chop.

2. Mix ground pork together well with green onion, ginger, salty egg white, mushroom, raw egg white, salt, sugar, soy sauce, cornstarch, sesame oil and 1-2 T. water.

3. Wipe oil inside steam proof bowl; lay salted preserved egg yolk in bottom. Add pork mixture. Place in steamer with water at full boil; steam for 10 minutes over high heat.

4. Remove and turn out upside down onto serving platter so egg yolk is on top.

Ingredients:

8 oz. bamboo shoot sliced thin

8 oz. lean boneless pork

3 oz. dried lily buds

2 slices ginger

2 stalks green onion, 1" pieces

1 t. salt

Sesame oil

Instructions:

1. Shred pork; soak lily buds to soften.
2. Bring 5 C. water to boil. Add bamboo shoots, pork, lily buds, green onion, and ginger slices. Cook for 10 minutes.
3. Season with salt; sprinkle with sesame oil and serve hot.

Ingredients:

8 oz. shrimp, shelled and cleaned

8 oz. oysters, shucked

8 oz. tuna (canned)

3 eggs

1 T. chopped green onion

1 t. chopped ginger

1 t. salt

1/2 T. cooking wine

3 T. oil

Instructions:

1. Add salt to raw oyster, mix well. Rinse clean. Add wine and ginger to shrimp and oyster; allow to marinate.

2. Mix eggs, 1-2 T. water and green onions and beat.

3. Heat oil. When hot, add shrimp, oyster and tuna and stir-fry evenly.

4. After seafood is nearly cooked, add egg mixture and cook until egg sets. Season with salt and serve hot.

Ingredients:

1 lb. pork intestine

2 stalks scallions, shredded

2 hot red peppers

1 t. chopped ginger

1/2 t. salt

1 t. sugar

1 1/2 T. hot pepper paste

1/2 T. cornstarch

3 T. oil

Instructions:

1. Sprinkle pork intestines with cornstarch and press. Rinse clean and shred into fine strips.
2. Heat oil. When hot, stir-fry ginger and hot pepper paste. Add pork and stir-fry evenly.
3. Add scallions and shredded hot peppers. Season with salt and sugar.
4. Thicken with cornstarch/water solution and serve hot.

Ingredients:

10 oz. round cabbage

8 oz. seasoned dried bean curd

2 T. chopped green onion

1 t. chopped red pepper

3 T. soy sauce

1 t. sugar

1/2 T. vinegar

1 t. sesame oil

Instructions:

1. Cut cabbage into bite-sized pieces; parboil. Remove and drain; cool.
2. Slice seasoned dried bean curd thinly. Parboil; remove, drain; cool.
3. Mix sugar with a small amount of warm water to dissolve.
4. Mix green onion, red pepper, soy sauce, sugar solution, vinegar and sesame oil thoroughly. Pour over cabbage and seasoned dried bean curd. Mix thoroughly and serve.

Ingredients:

10 oz. small clams

10 oz. spareribs, cut in 1" pieces

1 t. chopped fresh ginger

3 stalks green onion, 1" pieces

1 T. chopped green onion

1 1/2 t. salt

1 T. cooking wine

Instructions:

1. Parboil spareribs; remove. Soak clams in salted water so they are cleansed of sand.

2. Bring 5 C. water, spareribs, and green onion pieces to boil over high heat. Reduce heat and simmer for 30 minutes.

3. Raise heat, then add clams and ginger and cook until clams open.

4. Season with salt and wine. Sprinkle with chopped green onion and serve hot.

Ingredients:

10 oz. pork belly

10 oz. turnip

3 stalks green onion, 1" pieces

1 t. chopped ginger

1 T. chopped green onion

1/2 t. salt

1 t. sugar

4 T. soy sauce

1 T. cooking wine

1/2 C. oil

Instructions:

1. Cut peeled turnip into bite-sized pieces. Parboil pork belly; remove and cut into thick pieces.
2. Add chopped ginger, 1 T. soy sauce and wine to pork; allow to marinate.
3. Heat 1/2 C. oil. When hot, add pork belly and fry till lightly browned. Remove and drain.
4. Place pork belly, turnip, 3 T. soy sauce and green onion in 3 C. water and bring to boil over high heat. Reduce heat and simmer until turnip is soft and tender.
5. Reduce liquid and then season with salt and sugar. Sprinkle with chopped green onion and serve hot.

Ingredients:

6 chicken giblets

8 oz. snow peas

1 t. chopped ginger

1 T. chopped green onion

1 t. salt

1 t. sugar

1 1/2 T. soy sauce

1/2 T. cooking wine

3 T. oil

Instructions:

1. Cut each giblet in half. Remove skin and score flesh lightly. Parboil and remove.
2. Heat oil. When hot, stir-fry snow peas briefly and remove.
3. Stir-fry giblets in remaining oil; add ginger, green onion and soy sauce. Mix evenly and add snow peas.
4. Season with salt, sugar and wine. Serve hot.

Ingredients:

10 oz. bitter melon

3 oz. tiny dried fish

1 T. fermented salted black beans

3 stalks green onion, 1" sections

1 t. salt

1/2 T. cooking wine

3 T. oil

Instructions:

1. Remove seeds from bitter melon; slice into bite-sized pieces.
2. Soak black beans until soft.
3. Heat oil. When hot, stir-fry green onion and bitter melon. Add 1 C. water, fish and beans. Cook until water comes to a boil. Add salt to season.
4. Simmer over low heat for 15 minutes until bitter melon is soft. Sprinkle with wine and serve hot.

Ingredients:

6 oz. ground pork

8 oz. salted mustard root

8 oz. wild arum

1 T. chopped green onion

Several slices ginger

1/2 t. salt

Sesame oil

Instructions:

1. Bring salted mustard root and 5 C. water to a boil.
2. Add ginger slices, wild arum and pork to simmer for 10 minutes.
3. Season with salt; sprinkle with sesame oil and chopped green onion to serve.

Ingredients:

10 oz. pork intestines

8 oz. potatoes

Meat seasoning (such as "Shake n'Bake")

1 t. chopped ginger

1 T. chopped green onion

2 T. soy sauce

1 T. hot pepper paste

1/2 T. cooking wine

1 t. sugar

Instructions:

1. Rinse pork intestines with water until clean. Place in boiling water and cook for 30 minutes over low heat.
2. Peel potatoes and cut into 1" pieces.
3. Add ginger, soy sauce, hot pepper paste, sugar, wine, meat seasoning and a small amount of water to intestines. Mix evenly. Arrange at bottom of steam proof bowl; lay potato pieces on top.
4. Remove and turn out upside down onto serving platter. Sprinkle with chopped green onion and serve.

Ingredients:

6 chicken wings

1 cake bean curd

4 stalks green onion, shredded

1 t. chopped ginger

1 t. salt

1/2 T. soy sauce

1/2 T. cooking wine

1 T. oil

Instructions:

1. Cut bean curd into cubes.
2. Mix ginger, soy sauce, salt and wine; add to wings and mix evenly.
3. Place wings in steamer together with bean curd; steam for about 15 minutes. Remove to serving platter.
4. Heat 1 T. oil. When hot, add green onions and stir-fry lightly. Pour over bean curd and chicken and serve.

Ingredients:

1 yellow croaker, cleaned and scaled

8 oz. winter vegetables (preserved mustard greens)

3 stalks green onion, shredded

2 slices ginger

1 t. salt

1 t. sugar

2 T. soy sauce

1 T. cooking wine

3 T. oil

Instructions:

1. Heat frying pan with scant amount of oil; fry fish on both sides until lightly browned; remove.

2. Heat 3 T. oil. When hot, fry green onion and ginger, then add winter vegetable. Stir-fry briefly, then add 3 C. water, soy sauce, salt and sugar. Bring to boil.

3. Add fish; allow to simmer until some liquid has evaporated. Add wine and serve.

Ingredients:

1 lb. shrimp, shelled and cleaned

1 stalk celery, chopped

1 t. chopped ginger

2 stalks green onion, cut in strips

1 1/2 t. salt

1 T. cooking wine

1 T. cornstarch

1 egg white

Sesame oil

Black pepper

Instructions:

1. Chop shrimp. Add ginger, 1/2 t. salt, wine, cornstarch and egg white. Mix evenly to make ground shrimp mixture.
2. Bring 5 C. water to boil; form shrimp mixture into small balls and add to water. Add green onion; cook for 10 minutes.
3. Season with 1 t. salt; sprinkle with chopped celery and black pepper. Add a few drops of sesame oil and serve hot.

Author's Notes

We planned this "**Family Style**" cookbook with care because we wished to produce a book that is attractive and that can be read and understood easily for everyday use in the home.

Our main objective in creating this cookbook is to provide recipes for the working adult that are nutritious, economical and simple to prepare.

There is a guide at the beginning of "**Family Style**" that is designed to provide general knowledge of kitchen aesthetics and maintenance. We hope the reader finds the tips therein useful and informative.

Several more Chinese cookbooks are to be released in this series. If you enjoy "**Family Style**," I am sure you will be pleased with what is to follow!